The Chase

Anthony McGowan
Illustrated by Jon Stuart

OXFORD

In this story ...

Also look out for ...

Chapter 1 — Sweet dreams?

It was a hot summer's day and the children had been playing in the park. Tiger was snoozing in the cool shade of a tree. He dreamed that someone was tickling his wrist. It was really quite a nice feeling. Then he opened his eyes. He knew straight away that something was wrong. Tiger looked around him. He could see Max and Cat chatting. Max was showing Cat his new skateboard. Ant was also close by, reading a book. He was always reading. Tiger sometimes made fun of him, but he knew deep down that reading was cool.

His friends were all fine. So what was it then?
Why did he feel so strange? Did he have any
homework to do? No, for once he'd already
finished his homework. Perhaps it was time to
go home. He looked at his watch.

NO HE DIDN'T!

There wasn't a watch to look at! His wrist was
completely bare. His watch must have slipped
off when they were playing earlier. He looked
around frantically. There was no sign of it.

Max would be so angry. It was hard to make Max angry, but losing the watch might do it. Cat would definitely have a go at him. She could be pretty scary when she wanted to. Even Ant would probably go mad.

Then Tiger saw something ... a glint of shiny, green metal. An X-bot! It was heading towards a drain. And it was carrying his watch in its sharp steel jaws.

In a flash Tiger
realized what must have
happened. The X-bot had been
sent by the evil Dr X to steal the
watch. It must have crept up on
him as he dozed and unfastened the
strap. That was the tickling he had felt.

"Hey, come back here!" Tiger yelled.

The X-bot turned to look at him and then
hurried on. It slipped between the metal bars
of the grate covering the drain.

"What is it, Tiger?"

It was Max. He'd heard Tiger's shout.

"Quick, help," said Tiger. "It's got my watch!"

The others rushed up and Tiger explained
what had happened.

Chapter 2 — Scaredy Cat

➔ ➔ ➔ ➔ ➔ ➔ ➔ ➔ ➔ ➔ ➔ ➔ ➔ ➔ ➔ ➔ ➔ ➔

"We've got to get Tiger's watch back!" said Max.

"But how?" groaned Tiger. "That X-bot has taken it down the drain. I'll never see it again!"

"We will get it back," replied Max, firmly. "But we'll have to split up."

The others gathered closer to listen. Tiger really hoped Max would come up with one of his brilliant plans.

Max slipped off his rucksack and unzipped it. He took out a small flying machine that was made from a hand-held fan. It was their micro-copter.

Ant and Tiger smiled. Cat grimaced.

"Not that thing!" she said.

"This *thing* happens to be the latest in micro-flying technology," said Max, holding it up. He was very proud of his invention.

"Yeah, it's got plenty of leg room," said Ant, with a grin.

"Plenty of leg room!" said Cat.

"Can we get back to finding my watch please?" said Tiger anxiously.

"Yes, sorry, Tiger," said Max. He could tell Tiger was getting upset. "Right, Cat. You take the micro-copter."

"What? Me? No way!" she screeched. "I'm not going up in that contraption."

"Think about it, Cat. Your watch is the only one with the tracking function. You can lock on to Tiger's watch and follow exactly where the X-bot takes it."

Cat didn't like the plan very much, but she understood that the others needed her.

"OK, I'll do it," she said, reluctantly.

Max smiled and handed her the micro-copter.

"Now," said Max. "Tiger, you've lost your watch, so you can't shrink. You'll have to follow on my skateboard. Just keep Cat in sight, and you'll be right above us."

"OK," replied Tiger.

"That leaves you, Ant. You're coming with me down into the drains to track the X-bot on foot."

"Oh goody," said Ant, sarcastically, "so I get to play in the nice smelly drains. My mum will be pleased."

Max, Cat and Ant turned the dials on their watches. They pushed the X and ...

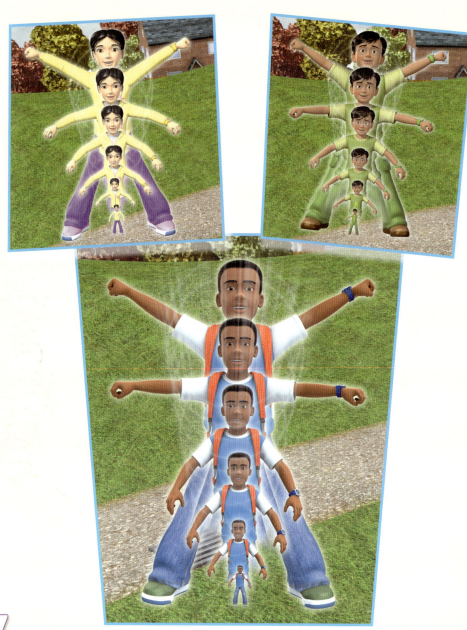

Chapter 3 — Take off!

Cat was terrified. She strapped herself into the micro-copter, desperately trying to remember what Max had told her. He had only given her a quick demonstration of how it worked. She pressed the starter button and the little engine roared into life. Well, to Cat it sounded like a roar. To anyone else who happened to be nearby it would have sounded exactly like the buzzing of a bee.

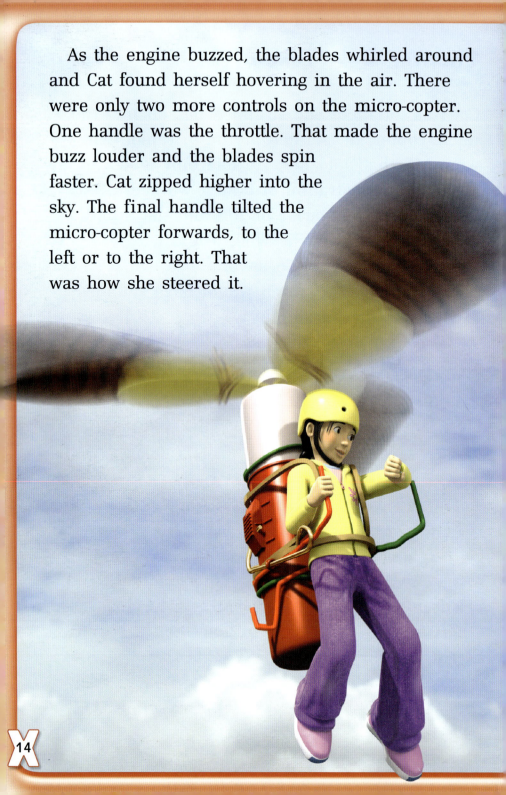

As the engine buzzed, the blades whirled around and Cat found herself hovering in the air. There were only two more controls on the micro-copter. One handle was the throttle. That made the engine buzz louder and the blades spin faster. Cat zipped higher into the sky. The final handle tilted the micro-copter forwards, to the left or to the right. That was how she steered it.

Cat checked her watch. She saw three lights. The green light for Ant and the blue for Max were moving forwards. Ahead of them was the red light for Tiger's watch, lost somewhere in the dark of the drains.

Even though she was nervous about being up in the air, she was secretly quite pleased that she wasn't down there in the smelly, slimy drains.

Below her, Tiger kicked off and the skateboard began to roll down the hill.

"Let's get to work," said Cat to herself, and she dipped the micro-copter in the direction of the red light.

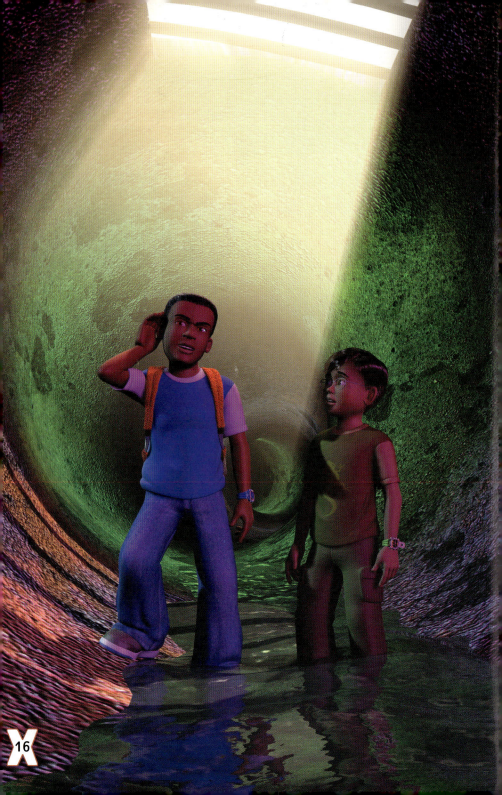

At the same moment, Max and Ant were lowering themselves into the drain. Max dropped down into the darkness. He landed with a splash.

"Everything OK?" asked Ant, nervously. His voice echoed in the dark.

"Fine," said Max. "Just a little bit of water down here. Your turn. I'll try to catch you."

Ant let go. He landed on Max and they both fell face down into the dirty brown ooze at the bottom of the drain.

"Yuck!" cried Ant. "I've been in here precisely four seconds and I'm already filthy."

"No time to worry about that now," said Max. "We've got to get after that X-bot."

"But how will we find it?" asked Ant.

"We listen," said Max.

They cupped their hands to their ears.

"Hear it?" said Max.

"No ..." replied Ant. "Wait, I hear something. There's a sort of tapping."

"Come on," said Max, starting to run.

As the micro-friends set off in hot pursuit of the X-bot thief, they did not notice that in a dark corner a pair of black eyes gleamed and a long, scaly tail swished from side to side.

Chapter 4 — Near miss

→ → → → → → → → → → → → → →

Tiger could just see Cat and the
micro-copter hovering in the blue
sky above. He was a fast skateboarder.
Max was more stylish and knew more tricks,
but Tiger was fearless. He sped along the path
through the park, weaving in and out of the
people – he had to keep Cat in sight.

Then he saw a man with a baby in a pushchair. The baby was crying. The man stopped suddenly and went to try to cheer the baby up. There was no room to go around them. Tiger had to veer off on to the grass. The skateboard hit a rock and Tiger went flying through the air. He landed in a crumpled heap in the bushes. He was glad that he had put on Max's helmet and kneepads. But there was no time to rub his bruises. He picked up the skateboard and ran back to the path. Then he was off again at top speed. The man with the pushchair hadn't even noticed him.

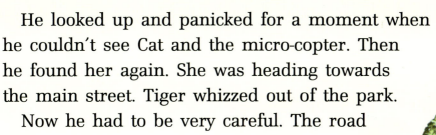

He looked up and panicked for a moment when he couldn't see Cat and the micro-copter. Then he found her again. She was heading towards the main street. Tiger whizzed out of the park.

Now he had to be very careful. The road was busy with cars and buses and the pavement was crowded with people doing their shopping.

Up above, Cat was still carefully tracking Tiger's watch. The X-bot was moving quickly along the tunnel. She looked down and tried to find Tiger. She was over the main street and it was hard to see him down there. She looked through the telescope on her watch and scanned the street again.

"There!" she said to herself. She had found him.

Cat was more confident now in the micro-copter. She looped-the-loop to let Tiger know where she was.

Chapter 5 — Boiled sweets

Down in the drains, Max and Ant were still running along. Every once in a while they stopped and listened to make sure that they could hear the tapping of the X-bot's metal feet, or the splashing as it went through a puddle.

There were horrible things down in the drains. Max tried to stay cheerful, but even he was finding it difficult as a big hairy spider crossed in front of them.

Max and Ant were so busy concentrating on what was ahead of them that they didn't notice the scratching of sharp claws behind them, or the sniffing pink nose …

Meanwhile ...

Tiger was quite impressed with the loop-the-loop Cat had performed. He looked down again, just in time to see an old lady up ahead, in front of him. He got ready to swerve around her. But then she dropped her bag of shopping. Everything fell out: bananas, bread, teabags, sugar, biscuits. The poor old lady let out a wail of despair.

Tiger could still have gone around her, but he felt sorry for the old lady. He jumped off the skateboard and helped her put the shopping back in the bag. He knew he had to be quick.

"There you go," he said, politely.

"Thank you so much," replied the old lady. "You're a very nice young man. Now, let me find something for you."

"Really, you don't have to," said Tiger, hurriedly.

He could still see the micro-copter, but only just. He was anxious to be off again. The old lady searched in her bag, and then in all her pockets, and then in her bag again. Finally she found what she was looking for – a packet of boiled sweets. It looked a very old packet, nearly as old as the lady herself.

"Here you are," she said, and picked him out an orange-flavoured one. Tiger didn't like boiled sweets, least of all orange ones. But he thanked her anyway and put it in his pocket.

He waved goodbye. Then he was off again, just in time to see Cat disappear around a corner.

Chapter 6 — Cat amongst the pigeons

Down in the drains, Max and Ant crept further down the tunnel. There was a faint red light ahead.

"Look," whispered Max.

"I think that's the light from Tiger's watch," replied Ant. "You can see the reflection on the X-bot's metal surface."

"I wonder where we are?" said Max.

"It's hard to keep track down here," replied Ant. "But we can't be far away from the NASTI headquarters."

"I think it's time to make our move."

"Good," said Ant, "I'm sick of these drains."

Just then a big gloop of green slime fell from the roof and splattered on to his back.

"Delightful," he sighed.

Up in the air ...

Cat zoomed round the corner in the micro-copter and plunged straight into a flock of pigeons. Wings beat the air all around her. The pigeons were as startled as she was. They were afraid of the buzzing engine and the whirring blades.

Cat threw the micro-copter violently from side to side trying to avoid the terrified birds. She didn't want to hurt them.

On the ground, Tiger tried to follow Cat's movements.

"What is she playing at?" he said to himself.

He turned this way and that, doubling back on himself and then shooting off in new directions, trying to keep up with Cat.

Finally Cat escaped from the pigeons. When she looked at her watch she was dismayed to find that she had lost the trail – there was no sign of the flashing lights that told her where the other watches were. But by now she knew where the X-bot was heading – to the NASTI headquarters, underneath the offices of the NICE building.

Chapter 7 — The charge

Underground, Max and Ant were now close enough to see the X-bot scurrying ahead of them through the drain. Behind them, the dark shape in the shadows was almost close enough to pounce.

"Right," hissed Max, "it's now or never."

"What's the plan?" said Ant.

"Plan? Oh, um, well ..."

The truth was that, for once, Max didn't really have a plan. He hadn't thought what they would do when they finally caught up with the X-bot.

AAAAHHHHHH!

"Yes?" asked Ant, still waiting.

"OK," said Max, quickly, "what we do, is run up to the X-bot and, er, get the watch back."

There was a pause and then Ant said: "You mean take it by surprise?"

"Yeah," said Max, "that's exactly what I meant." And with that, Max rushed towards the X-bot, screaming at the top of his voice. For a second, Ant stood by himself. Then he shrugged his shoulders, and followed Max, screaming just as loudly.

AAAAHHHHHH!

Up in the air, Cat was circling around the NICE building. She knew the X-bot must be somewhere around there. She hoped it hadn't reached the safety of NASTI. Suddenly, Cat heard a blip and looked at her watch.

"Yes," she shouted, "I've got you!"

All three lights were clustered together. She dipped the micro-copter and headed for the signal.

"At last!" exclaimed Tiger, as he saw Cat begin to descend. He had been doing his best to keep up with her, weaving through the street on the skateboard, but now he was getting tired. And he desperately wanted his watch back.

Chapter 8 — Surprise, surprise

The X-bot spun around to face the two charging children. Max was hoping that the surprise attack would make the X-bot drop the watch. Then they could grab it and run away. He knew that it was probably the lamest plan he'd ever had, but even a lame plan was better than no plan at all.

You couldn't really say that the X-bot smiled, because it didn't have lips, or any of the other things you need to smile, but something about the machine looked pleased to see Max and Ant. It definitely did not look surprised.

Max was puzzled for a moment. Then he realized why the X-bot looked happy. It wasn't alone. Behind the X-bot holding Tiger's watch, there was the glint of more metal bodies. There were three more X-bots.

"A trap!" Max shouted.

The X-bots moved towards the children.

"What shall we do?" yelled Ant.

Max felt terrible. He had led Ant into the trap, and now they would be captured for sure.

Then, before Max could say anything, the X-bot holding Tiger's watch really did look surprised. In fact, it looked more than surprised – it looked scared stiff. It dropped the watch.

Max and Ant spun round to see what the X-bot was looking at. It was a huge brown rat, with horrible yellow teeth. It leapt towards them.

The rat landed in the middle of the X-bots. They scattered. Max rushed forwards and grabbed the watch. He slung it over his shoulder.

"Run!" he screamed to Ant, and they both ran. Behind them the X-bots clanked and bleeped, and the rat squeaked and scratched.

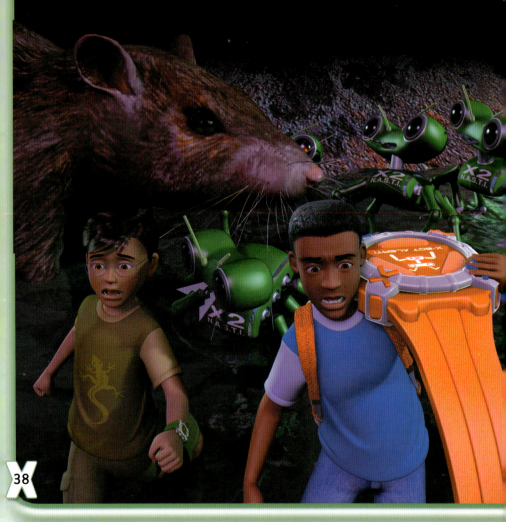

Up in the air, Cat saw the three watches come together and then move off again.

"Drat," she said, and turned the micro-copter to follow.

Underneath her, Tiger copied her move, just managing to swerve around a lamp post.

Cat saw a drain cover ahead. The lights on her watch were heading for it. She landed next to it and quickly unstrapped herself from the micro-copter. Then she turned the dial on her watch, pressed the X and grew back to normal size.

Tiger reached her, breathless.

"They're down there," said Cat, excitedly.

Tiger peered into the grate and shouted: "Ant, Max, we're here!"

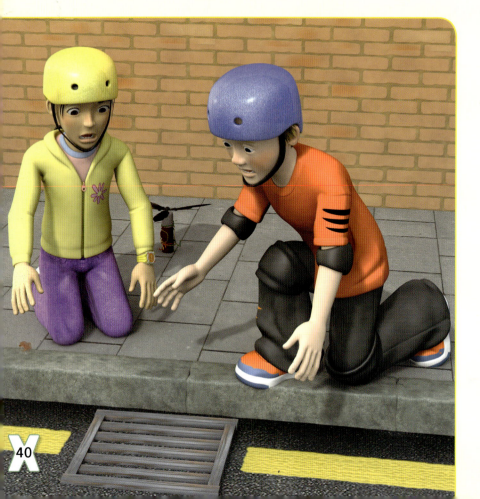

Chapter 9 — Light at the end of the tunnel

➡ ➡ ➡ ➡ ➡ ➡ ➡ ➡ ➡ ➡ ➡ ➡ ➡ ➡ ➡ ➡ ➡ ➡ ➡

Max and Ant were running as fast as they could. They could hear the sound of marching metal feet.

"They're after us," said Ant. "That poor old rat must have run away."

"That poor old rat wanted to eat us!" said Max.

"Maybe, but without it we'd never have got the watch."

It was then that they heard Tiger's shout and saw a light ahead. But the marching feet behind them were getting louder.

"There!" yelled Max. "We can make it."

They reached the light and looked up into Tiger's happy face. Tiger stretched his fingers down to help them out, but Max and Ant couldn't reach them.

"Your shoelace," said Cat, from over Tiger's shoulder.

"What?"

"Your shoelace ... they can climb up it."

"Please hurry," said Ant. "The X-bots are nearly here. They'll get *all* the watches!"

Tiger ripped the lace from one of his trainers and dropped one end down to Max and Ant.

Max was brilliant at climbing ropes and, even though he was carrying the heavy watch, he got to the top in no time at all. He blinked in the sunlight, then turned the dial on his watch and pressed the X to grow back to normal size.

A sad cry came from down in the drain.

"Help, I can't do it!"

Ant was struggling to climb the shoelace.

"Tie it around your waist," yelled Tiger.

Ant fumbled with the lace. It felt very thick and heavy. The X-bots scuttled forwards. At the last moment Ant finished tying the knot.

"Now!" he shrieked.

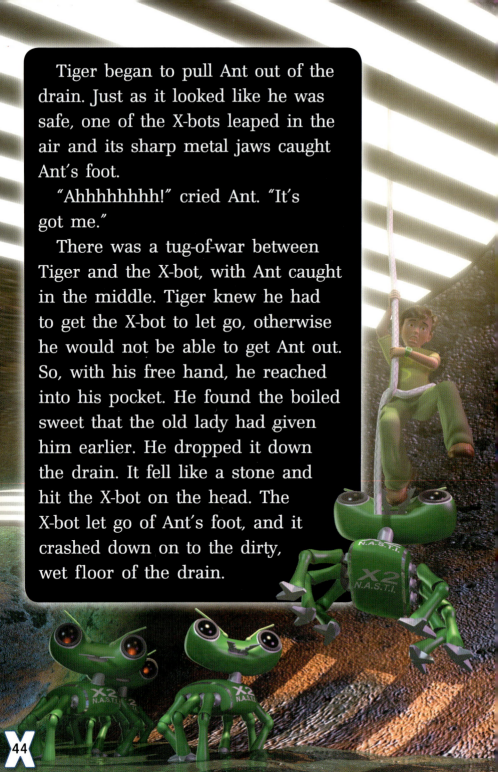

Tiger began to pull Ant out of the drain. Just as it looked like he was safe, one of the X-bots leaped in the air and its sharp metal jaws caught Ant's foot.

"Ahhhhhhhh!" cried Ant. "It's got me."

There was a tug-of-war between Tiger and the X-bot, with Ant caught in the middle. Tiger knew he had to get the X-bot to let go, otherwise he would not be able to get Ant out. So, with his free hand, he reached into his pocket. He found the boiled sweet that the old lady had given him earlier. He dropped it down the drain. It fell like a stone and hit the X-bot on the head. The X-bot let go of Ant's foot, and it crashed down on to the dirty, wet floor of the drain.

Tiger pulled Ant into the sunlight, and a grinning Ant turned the dial and pressed the X on his watch.

The four friends stood together, tired but happy.

"We made it," said Max.

"Thanks, everyone," said Tiger. "You saved my watch."

"Yes, but you and Cat saved us," Ant replied.

"When we're a team, nothing can beat us," said Max, and they all cheered.

Then Max and Ant went home for a bath!

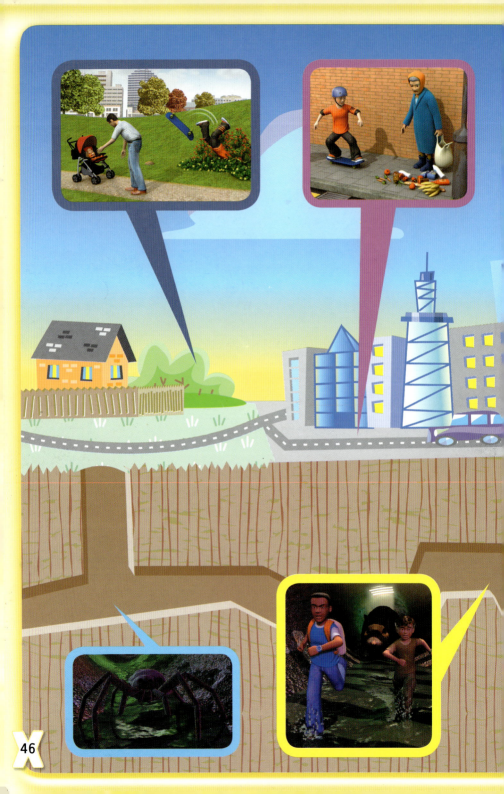

Foiled Again!

Find out more ...

For more fast and furious adventures read ...

The Super Skateplank

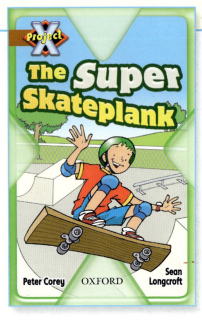

and *The Fun Run*